Collins

AQA GCSE 9-1
Sociology
Workbook

Pauline Wilson

Revision That Really Works

Experts have discovered that there are two techniques that help you to retain and recall information and consistently produce better results in exams compared to other revision techniques.

It really isn't rocket science either – you simply need to:

- **test yourself** on each topic as many times as possible
- **leave a gap** between the test sessions.

Three Essential Revision Tips

1. Use Your Time Wisely

- Allow yourself plenty of time.
- Try to start revising at least six months before your exams – it's more effective and less stressful.
- Don't waste time re-reading the same information over and over again – it's not effective!

2. Make a Plan

- Identify all the topics you need to revise.
- Plan at least five sessions for each topic.
- One hour should be ample time to test yourself on the key ideas for a topic.
- Spread out the practice sessions for each topic – the optimum time to leave between each session is about one month but, if this isn't possible, just make the gaps as big as you can.

3. Test Yourself

- Methods for testing yourself include: quizzes, practice questions, flashcards, past papers, explaining a topic to someone else, etc.
- Don't worry if you get an answer wrong – provided you check what the correct answer is, you are more likely to get the same or similar questions right in future!

Visit **collins.co.uk/collinsGCSErevision** for more information about the benefits of these revision techniques, and for further guidance on how to plan ahead and make them work for you.

Command Words used in Exam Questions

This table defines some of the most commonly used command words in GCSE exam questions.

Command word	Meaning
Identify...	State a point briefly or name
Describe...	Set out the main features or characteristics; give an account of
From Item B...	Draw on relevant material – but do not just copy it out!
Identify and explain one reason why...	Briefly state a relevant reason and develop this by discussing the reason in more depth
Discuss how far sociologists would agree that...	Explain one side of the debate and assess it. Present other sides of the debate and assess them. Come to a conclusion on 'how far'.

Contents

Topic-based Questions

Practice Exam Papers

GCSE Sociology Workbook

Families

Different Family Forms

1 Which term is commonly used by sociologists to describe families in which one or both partners have a child or children from a previous relationship living with them?
Shade **one** box only. [1]

A Blended family   ○

B Conventional family   ○

C Extended family   ○

D Nuclear family   ○

2 Describe **one** stage in the family life-cycle. [3]

....

....

....

....

....

....

....

Families

The Functions of Families

3 Discuss how far sociologists would agree that nuclear families perform vital functions in
British society today.   [12]

Continue your answer on a separate piece of paper.

Families

The Marxist Perspective on Families

4 Identify and explain **one** advantage of using unstructured interviews to investigate married people's experience of marriage and family life. [4]

Feminist and Other Critical Views of Families

5 Identify and explain **one** criticism that feminist sociologists make about the nuclear family. [4]

Continue your answer on a separate piece of paper.

Families

Conjugal Role Relationships

6 Describe the conventional family. [3]

Changing Relationships Within Families

Item A

Young and Willmott (1973) attempted to trace the development of the family from pre-industrial Britain to the present using a mixed methods approach including historical research and a social survey. The survey questionnaire took the form of a structured interview, with questions on the house, car, occupation, work, leisure, home and family life.

Young and Willmott's findings suggested that the symmetrical family had become the typical family form in Britain. They described symmetrical relationships as opposite but similar. So, although the husband and wife carried out opposite or different tasks, each made a similar contribution to the home. Decision-making, including financial decisions, was more shared and family members spent more of their leisure time together in the home.

7 From **Item A**, examine **one** weakness of the research. [2]

Families

8 Identify and explain **one** factor that may account for the move to the symmetrical family, as referred to in **Item A**. [4]

Changing Family and Household Structures

9 Identify and describe **one** way in which households in Britain have changed since the 1970s. [3]

Families

Marriage and Divorce

10 Which term is used by sociologists to describe a marriage in which a man has two or more wives at the same time? Shade **one** box only.   [1]

A   Monogamy   ○   B   Polyandry   ○

C   Polygamy   ○   D   Polygyny   ○

Item B

Data from the Office for National Statistics (ONS) show that, in 1973, there were 8.4 divorces per 1000 married men and 8.4 per 1000 married women in England and Wales. In general, the divorce rate increased over the next 20 years and, in 1993, the figures stood at 14.3 for men and 14.1 for women.

In 2013, however, there were just 9.8 divorces per 1000 married men and 9.8 per 1000 married women. These rates are similar to the divorce rates in the mid-1970s.

---

11 From **Item B**, examine **one** strength of the data.   [2]

....

....

....

....

....

12 Identify the type of data referred to in **Item B**. Explain **one** factor that may account for the increase in the divorce rate between 1973 and 1993.   [4]

....

....

....

....

....

Continue your answer on a separate piece of paper.

Education

The Role of Education from a Functionalist Perspective

1 Identify and explain **one** function of education. [4]

The Marxist Approach to Education

2 Discuss how far sociologists would agree that the main role of education is to meet the needs of capitalism. [12]

Continue your answer on a separate piece of paper.

Education

Different Types of School

3 Describe **one** form of educational provision that is an alternative to school-based education.

[3]

....

....

....

....

....

....

....

....

4 Identify and describe **one** possible criticism of the tripartite system.

[3]

....

....

....

....

....

....

....

....

Education

Social Class and Educational Achievement

Item A

In 2016, the Sutton Trust published a research report on private tuition in England and Wales. The report drew on a poll carried out by an opinion poll company for the Sutton Trust. The poll asked young people aged 11–16 years about the experience of receiving private tuition. The sample size was 2555 students.

The report also drew on data from other sources including the UK Millennium Cohort Study which had a sample size of 19 000 children aged 11 years.

The Sutton Trust reported that affluent families were more likely to employ private tutors for their children than less affluent families. Children attending private schools were around twice as likely to have private tuition as children attending state schools.

In England and Wales over the last decade, the proportion of young people who have received private tuition rose from 18 per cent to 25 per cent.

Source: adapted from http://www.suttontrust.com

---

5 From **Item A**, examine **one** strength of the research. [2]

....

....

....

....

....

....

Education

6 Describe the change in the proportion of young people who had private tuition, as referred to in **Item A**. Explain **one** factor that might account for this change.   [4]

....

....

....

....

....

....

....

....

....

....

The Impact of School Processes on Working-Class Students' Achievements

7 Identify and explain **one** disadvantage of using a longitudinal study to investigate the effects of banding in schools.   [4]

....

....

....

....

....

....

....

....

Education

Ethnicity and Educational Achievement

8 Which term is commonly used by sociologists to describe a curriculum that judges one culture (such as white, European culture) as superior to others? Shade **one** box only.   [1]

A Biased curriculum   ◯   B Ethnocentric curriculum   ◯

C Informal curriculum   ◯   D Official curriculum   ◯

9 Identify and describe **one** possible example of institutional racism within schools.   [3]

....

....

....

....

....

....

....

....

....

Gender and Educational Achievement

10 Identify and describe **one** criticism that some feminists make of the curriculum in schools.   [3]

....

....

....

....

....

....

Continue your answer on a separate piece of paper.

Education

Perspectives on the Counter-School Culture

11 Which term is used by sociologists to describe the study of people in everyday settings?
Shade **one** box only. [1]

A Covert observation ◯

B Ethnographic study ◯

C Longitudinal study ◯

D Survey ◯

12 Identify **one** ethical issue that you would need to consider when investigating a counter-school culture and explain how you would deal with this issue in your investigation. [4]

Crime and Deviance

An Introduction to Crime and Deviance

1 Identify **one** agency of formal social control and explain how it operates. [4]

Functionalist and Interactionist Perspectives on Crime and Deviance

2 Identify and explain **one** advantage of using participant observation to investigate deviant careers. [4]

Continue your answer on a separate piece of paper.

Crime and Deviance

3 Which term is used by sociologists to describe a situation in which the norms that regulate people's behaviour in society break down?

Shade **one** box only. [1]

A Anomie ⬭

B Anti-social behaviour ⬭

C Delinquency ⬭

D Media amplification ⬭

Marxist and Feminist Explanations of Crime and Deviance

4 Describe **one** way in which women are controlled in public. [3]

....

....

....

....

....

....

....

Statistical Data on the Extent of Crime

5 Identify and explain **one** problem with police-recorded crime statistics. [4]

....

....

....

....

....

Continue your answer on a separate piece of paper.

Crime and Deviance

Factors Affecting Criminal and Deviant Behaviour

6 Identify **one** ethical issue that you would need to consider when investigating young offenders and explain how you would deal with this issue in your investigation. [4]

Other Factors Affecting Criminal and Deviant Behaviour

7 Identify and explain **one** reason for women's increased involvement in crime in Britain since the 1970s. [4]

Continue your answer on a separate piece of paper.

Crime and Deviance

8 Which term is used by sociologists to describe the deal that offers material and emotional rewards to women in return for living with a male breadwinner within a family? Shade **one** box only. [1]

A Gender roles ⃝   B Class deal ⃝

C Role conflict ⃝   D Gender deal ⃝

9 Discuss how far sociologists would agree that different ethnic groups have similar experiences of the criminal justice system in Britain today. [12]

_____

_____

_____

_____

_____

_____

_____

_____

_____

_____

_____

_____

_____

_____

_____

_____

Continue your answer on a separate piece of paper.

Crime and Deviance

The Media and Public Debates over Crime

10 Describe **one** way in which the media set the agenda in relation to crime. [3]

_____

_____

_____

_____

_____

_____

_____

11 Identify and describe **one** example of a folk devil. [3]

_____

_____

_____

_____

_____

_____

_____

Social Stratification

An Introduction to Social Stratification

1. Which term is commonly used by sociologists to describe the way society is structured into a hierarchy of unequal layers?
Shade **one** box only. [1]

A Social class ⬭   B Social inequality ⬭

C Social stratification ⬭   D Social status ⬭

Different Views of Social Class

2. Which term is commonly used by sociologists to describe how people see or identify themselves in social class terms? Shade **one** box only. [1]

A False class consciousness ⬭   B Market situation ⬭

C Socio-economic class ⬭   D Subjective class ⬭

Factors Affecting Life Chances

3. Describe **one** way in which governments have tried to tackle racial discrimination in employment.   [3]

Social Stratification

4 Identify and describe **one** example of ageism.   [3]

....

....

....

....

....

....

....

Item A

Irene Zempi and Neil Chakraborti (2014) studied the experiences of Muslim women who wore the niqab (a face covering or veil) in public places in Leicester. The research was based on 60 semi-structured interviews with veiled Muslim women. In addition, one of the researchers, Irene Zempi (who describes herself as a white, Orthodox Christian woman) wore a veil in public places such as on public transport, in shopping centres and on the streets of Leicester for four weeks. This allowed her to understand more fully the women's experiences as victims of Islamophobia (hostility towards Muslims and Islam) in their daily lives.

For veiled Muslim women, the fear of being attacked and incidents of victimisation can have significant consequences such as loss of confidence and depression. It can also limit Muslim women's movements, leading to social isolation.

---

5 From **Item A**, examine **one** strength of the research.   [2]

....

....

....

....

....

Social Stratification

6 From **Item A**, examine **one** weakness of the research. [2]

_____

_____

_____

_____

_____

_____

7 Identify and explain **one** way in which religious hate crime might affect people's life chances, as experienced by many of the women referred to in **Item A**. [4]

_____

_____

_____

_____

_____

_____

_____

_____

_____

_____

_____

Social Stratification

Studies of Affluent Workers

8 Which term is used by sociologists to describe a process in which working-class families are becoming middle class in their norms and values as their incomes and standard of living improve? Shade **one** box only. [1]

A Affluence ○   B Assimilation ○

C Class alignment ○   D Embourgeoisement ○

9 Which term is used by sociologists to describe a family whose lifestyle and social relationships focus on the home and immediate family rather than on work and the extended family? Shade **one** box only. [1]

A Blended family ○   B Conventional family ○

C Dual career family ○   D Privatised nuclear family ○

10 Identify and describe **one** type of social mobility. [3]

....

....

....

....

....

....

....

....

Social Stratification

Wealth, Income and Poverty

11 Identify and explain **one** advantage of using official statistics to investigate poverty in the UK.   [4]

_____

_____

_____

_____

_____

_____

_____

_____

_____

Social Stratification

Different Explanations of Poverty

12 Discuss how far sociologists would agree that poverty results from class-based divisions in capitalist society.

[12]

Continue your answer on a separate piece of paper.

Social Stratification

Power and Authority

13 Describe **one** example of the use of power based on coercion.   [3]

....

....

....

....

....

....

....

14 Identify and explain **one** type of authority.   [4]

....

....

....

....

....

....

....

....

....

Social Stratification

Power and the State

15 From a Marxist perspective, identify **one** group that holds power in society and describe the source of its power.

[3]

Collins

GCSE Sociology

Paper 1 The Sociology of Families and Education

Time allowed: 1 hour 45 minutes

The maximum mark for this paper is 100.

Instructions

- Use black ink or black ball-point pen.
- Answer **all** questions.
- You must answer the questions in the spaces provided. Do **not** write outside the box around each page or on blank pages.
- Do all rough work in this book.

Information

- The marks for questions are shown in brackets.
- Questions should be answered in continuous prose. You will be assessed on your ability to:
  - use good English
  - organise information clearly
  - use specialist vocabulary where appropriate.

Name: _____

Section A: Families
Answer all questions in this section.

---

0 1 Which term is used by sociologists to describe one of the functions of families? Shade **one** box only.

A   Geographical mobility   ◯

B   Idealisation   ◯

C   Isolation   ◯

D   Reproduction   ◯   **[1 mark]**

0 2 Which term is commonly used by sociologists to describe a family in which power is held by a man? Shade **one** box only.

A   Dysfunctional family   ◯

B   Matriarchal family   ◯

C   Patriarchal family   ◯

D   Reconstituted family   ◯   **[1 mark]**

0 3 Describe **one** possible consequence of divorce for family members.   **[3 marks]**

....

....

....

....

....

....

| 0 | 4 | Identify and describe **one** alternative to the family. [3 marks]

Item A

The *Understanding Society* COVID-19 Study
The COVID-19 study is part of *Understanding Society*, a large-scale longitudinal study of households in the UK. The COVID-19 study was based on an online questionnaire. However, telephone interviews were carried out with people in households that did not use the internet regularly. The first wave of fieldwork began in April 2020 and the ninth and final wave began in September 2021. The COVID-19 study examined people's experiences of, and reactions to, the COVID-19 pandemic, covering topics such as family, education and health.
Data from the first wave of the COVID-19 study showed gender differences in the time spent by parents in the UK on housework, childcare and home schooling. For example, on average, employed mothers who were furloughed (on temporary leave from paid work due to coronavirus) spent 21 hours per week on housework. Employed fathers on furlough spent, on average, 12 hours weekly on housework.

| 0 | 5 | From **Item A**, examine **one** strength of the research. [2 marks]

....

....

....

0 6 Describe the difference in the hours spent on housework by mothers and fathers, shown in **Item A**. Explain **one** factor that might account for this difference.   **[4 marks]**

....

....

....

....

....

....

....

....

....

0 7 Identify and explain **one** advantage of using focus groups to investigate parents' experiences of home schooling.   **[4 marks]**

....

....

....

....

....

....

....

....

....

....

Item B

In her article on conventional families, Ann Oakley (1982) drew on evidence from research carried out by other sociologists. She argues that conventional nuclear family life is no longer the norm in statistical terms. Yet the idea of the conventional family is still a powerful one in society. People expect conventional family life to bring them happiness.

However, Oakley argues that there are strains beneath the surface. This is seen, for example, in the health problems and depression experienced by family members.

0 8 From **Item B**, identify and describe the research method used by Ann Oakley, including what you know of her perspective on the family. **[4 marks]**

....

....

....

....

....

....

....

0 9 Identify **one** ethical issue you would need to consider when investigating care of the elderly in Britain and explain how you would deal with this issue in your investigation. **[4 marks]**

1 0 Discuss how far sociologists would agree that the family serves the interests of capitalism in Britain today. **[12 marks]**

Practice Exam Paper 1

1 1 Discuss how far sociologists would agree that the nuclear family has become isolated from the wider family in British society. **[12 marks]**

Practice Exam Paper 1

Turn over for the next question.

Section B: Education
Answer all questions in this section.

---

1 2 Which term is commonly used by sociologists to describe schools in which the intake is based on an entry requirement such as passing an entrance examination? Shade **one** box only.

A Comprehensive schools ○

B Selective schools ○

C Specialist schools ○

D State schools ○ **[1 mark]**

1 3 Which term is used by sociologists to describe the learning that takes place in settings such as schools where people gain knowledge and skills across a range of subjects? Shade **one** box only.

A Formal education ○

B Hidden curriculum ○

C Informal education ○

D Official education ○ **[1 mark]**

1 4 Identify and describe **one** way in which education could facilitate social mobility. **[3 marks]**

....

....

....

....

....

....

....

....

....

1 5 Describe the crisis of masculinity that some males may experience. **[3 marks]**

....

....

....

....

....

....

....

....

Item C

> With SATs, the stakes are seen as high partly because the results contribute to the ranking of schools in league tables. Alice Bradbury (2021) and her colleagues explored how primary schools organised pupils for the high-stakes Year 6 SATs. The researchers carried out in-depth interviews with 20 primary school headteachers in different parts of England and a nationwide online survey of 288 headteachers. They also drew on official statistics from the Department for Education (DfE).
>
> Bradbury and her colleagues looked at the impact of SATs on classroom practices in primary schools. They found that some schools responded to the SATs by grouping pupils by ability into sets e.g. in maths and English. In some cases, headteachers objected to setting but felt that SATs encouraged it. Some schools targeted resources at the pupils who were on the borderline of meeting the expected standard and gave them extra help. However, this could be damaging if it meant other pupils got less attention.

1 6 From **Item C**, examine **one** strength of the research.   **[2 marks]**

1 7 Identify and explain **one** factor that might account for the way some primary schools responded to the SATs, as referred to in **Item C**.   **[4 marks]**

| 1 | 8 | Identify and explain **one** disadvantage of using a snowball sample to investigate an anti-school sub-culture among students in a secondary school. **[4 marks]**

Item D

Stephen Ball (1981) studied the impact of banding on students' experiences of schooling in a mixed comprehensive school. He undertook an intensive case study of one school, observing lessons, participating in the school's daily life as a supply teacher and teaching some timetabled lessons as a regular teacher. The field work was carried out over a period of more than two years.

Ball took notes during his observation of lessons and wrote these up as transcripts. He also kept diary notes to record his observations.

1 9 From **Item D**, identify and describe the research method used by Ball, including what you know of his perspective on education. **[4 marks]**

2 0 Identify **one** expectation that some teachers might have of students in the bottom band and explain how this might impact on the students' educational achievements. **[4 marks]**

Practice Exam Paper 1

2 1 Discuss how far sociologists would agree that home background is the most important factor in explaining differences in students' educational achievements. **[12 marks]**

Turn over for the next question.

2 2 Discuss how far sociologists would agree that government policies are the main reason for the improvements in the educational attainments of girls over the last 40 years.   **[12 marks]**

End of questions

Collins

GCSE Sociology

Paper 2 The Sociology of Crime and Deviance and Social Stratification

Time allowed: 1 hour 45 minutes

The maximum mark for this paper is 100.

Instructions

- Use black ink or black ball-point pen.
- Answer **all** questions.
- You must answer the questions in the spaces provided. Do **not** write outside the box around each page or on blank pages.
- Do all rough work in this book.

Information

- The marks for questions are shown in brackets.
- Questions should be answered in continuous prose. You will be assessed on your ability to:
  - use good English
  - organise information clearly
  - use specialist vocabulary where appropriate.

Name: _____

Section A: Crime and Deviance
Answer **all** questions in this section.

`0 1` Which term is used by sociologists to describe a group that is defined as a threat to society's values? Shade **one** box only.

A Folk devil ○

B Moral panic ○

C Pressure group ○

D Subculture ○ **[1 mark]**

`0 2` Which term is used by sociologists to describe crimes committed by employees on behalf of the company or organisation they work for? Shade **one** box only.

A Miscarriage of justice ○

B White-collar crime ○

C Indictable offences ○

D Corporate crime ○ **[1 mark]**

`0 3` Describe **one** way in which the media can amplify deviance. **[3 marks]**

....

....

....

....

....

....

....

....

....

0 4 Identify and describe **one** informal method of social control.   **[3 marks]**

....

....

....

....

....

....

....

Item A

Rachel Swann (2021) studied women's aggressive behaviour in pubs, bars and clubs in a city centre in Wales. She focused on a group of 78 white, working-class women aged between 18 and 58 years.

Swann used several methods to collect data. These included eight focus groups involving 45 women, six semi-structured interviews, and observations over a period of 16 months in the venues that the women went to.

Verbal aggression was commonplace but not all the women engaged in physical aggression. Swann explored how their behaviour made sense to them. She found that the women had their own rules about what they saw as appropriate behaviour. They saw their aggression as justified or necessary when the shared values and norms of their group (such as loyalty and respect) were broken.

0 5 From **Item A**, examine **one** strength of the research. **[2 marks]**

0 6 Identify and explain **one** reason why some sociologists explore how group members make sense of their own behaviour, as referred to in **Item A**. **[4 marks]**

0 7 Identify and explain **one** advantage of using a self-report study to investigate people's involvement in anti-social behaviour. **[4 marks]**

_____

_____

_____

_____

_____

_____

_____

_____

_____

_____

Item B

> **Strain and anomie**
>
> Merton (1938) argued that people's aspirations and goals are mainly determined by the values of their culture. But some individuals and groups end up experiencing strain between these goals and the means of achieving them.
>
> In this situation, where there is a mismatch between the goals and the means, a condition of anomie or normlessness develops. When this happens, the norms that regulate behaviour break down and people turn to whatever means work for them to achieve success.
>
> Merton identifies five possible ways that individuals respond to success goals in society. Some of these responses (such as innovation and retreatism) involve crime or deviance.

0 8 From **Item B,** identify and describe **one** response to success goals, including what you know of Merton's perspective on crime and deviance. **[4 marks]**

_____

_____

_____

_____

_____

_____

_____

_____

_____

0 9 Identify and explain **one** function of crime. **[4 marks]**

_____

_____

_____

_____

_____

_____

_____

1 0 Discuss how far sociologists would agree that the main cause of crime and deviance among young people is membership of a delinquent subculture. **[12 marks]**

Practice Exam Paper 2

1 1 Discuss how far sociologists would agree that official statistics on crimes recorded by the police do not provide an accurate measurement of crimes committed by females. **[12 marks]**

Practice Exam Paper 2

Section B: Social Stratification
Answer all questions in this section.

1 2 Which term is commonly used by sociologists to describe social positions that are fixed at birth? Shade **one** box only.

A   Achieved status   ◯

B   Ascribed status   ◯

C   Caste system   ◯

D   Social mobility   ◯   **[1 mark]**

1 3 Which term is used by sociologists to refer to the concentration of political power in the hands of an individual or a small group who rule by force? Shade **one** box only.

A   Censorship   ◯

B   Dictatorship   ◯

C   Pluralism   ◯

D   Traditional authority   ◯   **[1 mark]**

1 4 Describe **one** function of social stratification.   **[3 marks]**

....

....

....

....

....

....

1 5 Identify and describe **one** example of a voting system. [3 marks]

Item C

Charles Murray (1984) is an American political scientist and New Right thinker. He examined US governments' social policy and welfare programmes since the late 1960s that aimed to reduce poverty in the USA. He focused on the impact of these policies on the behaviour of members of the underclass. In his view, the policies actually produced poverty and encouraged more people to depend on welfare benefits.

Murray also carried out research on the underclass in the UK. He drew on trends shown in official statistics on crime rates, unemployment rates and births outside marriage to identify an emerging underclass. He argued that the underclass in the UK was growing rapidly. In his view, welfare reform encouraged crime, single parenthood and unemployment. It also took away the incentive to work.

1 6 From **Item C**, examine **one** weakness of the research. **[2 marks]**

....

....

....

....

....

1 7 Identify and explain **one** way in which governments' policies might produce poverty, as referred to in **Item C**. **[4 marks]**

....

....

....

....

....

....

....

1 8 Identify and explain **one** problem that sociologists might face when investigating social mobility in Britain. **[4 marks]**

Practice Exam Paper 2

Item D

Peter Townsend (1979) investigated how many people were living in poverty in the UK, their characteristics and problems. He used a large-scale questionnaire survey and collected data on 2052 households and 6098 individuals. The national questionnaire survey covered household resources and standards of living.

Townsend calculated that almost 23 per cent of the population were in poverty. He identified particular groups of people who were at risk of poverty. These included elderly people who had worked in unskilled manual jobs, and children in families of young unskilled manual workers or in one-parent families.

1 9 From **Item D**, identify and describe the research method used by Peter Townsend, including what you know of his perspective on poverty. **[4 marks]**

2 0 Identify and explain **one** factor that might have an impact on the life chances of young people. [4 marks]

2 1 Discuss how far sociologists would agree that social class is the most significant source of inequality in British society today. **[12 marks]**

Turn over for the next question.

2 2 Discuss how far sociologists would agree that the distribution of power in Britain is unequal.

[12 marks]

End of questions

There are no questions printed on this page.

Answers

Different Family Forms

1. A
2. **Suggested answer:** Rapoport and Rapoport saw empty nest families as one of the stages in the family life-cycle. An empty nest family is made up of a couple (e.g. a retired or middle-age couple) who live together. Their adult children have left the family home (flown the nest) so the couple's lifestyle and concerns are different compared to when their children were younger. **[Maximum 3 marks]**

The Functions of Families

3. **Possible content: up to 4 marks for AO1; up to 4 marks for AO2; up to 4 marks for AO3.**
   - Define the terms nuclear family and function. Indicate that the traditional nuclear family is declining in statistical terms.
   - Draw on the functionalist perspective (e.g. Murdock and Parsons) to argue that the nuclear family performs vital functions for individuals and society. Murdock (1949) identified four vital functions: sexual, reproductive, economic and educational. Parsons (1956) identified two vital functions: primary socialisation and stabilisation of adult personalities.
   - Criticise the functionalist approach e.g. it is outdated; it ignores diversity; it ignores functional alternatives to the nuclear family; it ignores dysfunctional families.
   - Draw on Marxist perspectives (e.g. Zaretsky) to argue that the nuclear family has an economic function that serves the interests of capitalism. In this sense, nuclear families are vital to capitalism. Marxists also argue that, through its socialisation function, the nuclear family is vital to the workings of capitalism.
   - Criticise the Marxist approach e.g. it ignores people's satisfaction with family life.
   - Draw on feminist perspectives (e.g. Delphy and Leonard) to argue that the patriarchal nuclear family is vital in the sense that it maintains patriarchal society.
   - Criticise the feminist approach e.g. it ignores egalitarian families.
   - Reach a balanced conclusion that addresses 'how far'.

The Marxist Perspective on Families

4. **Example answer:** Flexibility of unstructured interviews as a research method. **[1]** If a sociologist wants to get rich, detailed data about married people's unique experiences of marriage and family life, unstructured interviews would work well because they are flexible. They are not based on a long list of pre-set questions. A skilled interviewer could ask probing questions e.g. about an interviewee's children leaving home, the birth of a grandchild or the impact of unemployment on their marriage and family life. The interviewer could also ask follow-up questions to get a better understanding. This flexibility means that unstructured interviews may generate fresh ideas about people's experiences of marriage and family life. **[3] Other possible advantages:** The ability to build rapport with the research participants; interviewees can discuss their experiences in their own terms; validity of the data – **1 mark for a relevant advantage and 3 marks for explaining this advantage.**

Feminist and Other Critical Views of Families

5. **Example answer:** Delphy and Leonard criticise the nuclear family in patriarchal society because it is based on the economic exploitation of women. **[1]** This is because men benefit from the unpaid domestic work (housework and childcare) that women do within families for their husbands and other family members. Women are being exploited and oppressed because this work is neither valued nor paid. **[3] Other possible criticisms:** Unequal power relationships in nuclear families; domestic violence in nuclear families; financial inequality in nuclear families; women's double shift / triple burden in nuclear families – **1 mark for a relevant criticism and 3 marks for explaining this criticism.**

Conjugal Role Relationships

6. **Suggested answer:** Ann Oakley described the conventional family as a traditional nuclear family (a married couple and their children) who all live together. Roles and expectations are traditional and gendered. The wife is expected to do the unpaid domestic work within the home while the husband is expected to do the paid work outside the home. The husband's income gives him economic power but the wife is financially dependent on her husband. **[Maximum 3 marks]**

Changing Relationships Within Families

7. **Example answer:** One weakness is the interviewer effect. For example, if a young woman was interviewing the husband, he might exaggerate how much ironing he did to create a good impression. **[1]** Because the questions in a structured interview are all fixed, the interviewer cannot ask any probing questions about who does the ironing. So, the interview data and the findings about the symmetrical family may be invalid. **[1] Other possible weaknesses:** Interview bias; unequal power relationships; the research will generate statistics rather than qualitative data about people's lived experiences – **1 mark for a possible weakness and 1 mark for giving a reason why this is a weakness.**

8. **Example answer:** New equality legislation: in the 1970s legal changes came about with the Equal Pay Act (1970) and the Sex Discrimination Act (1975). **[1]** These laws protected women from being treated less favourably than men and gave them more equality and status at work. This could lead women to expect or demand equal relationships with their husbands in the home e.g. more equal conjugal roles and equality in decision-making. So, legal changes in the public sphere could affect attitudes and expectations in the private sphere. **[3] Other possible factors:** The impact of feminism; birth control enabling women to combine motherhood and paid work; technological developments leading to more home-based leisure activities – **1 mark for a relevant factor and 3 marks for explaining this factor.**

Changing Family and Household Structures

9. **Suggested answer:** One way in which households have changed is that the number of households containing just one person has increased. These one-person households often contain a younger person living alone e.g. singletons, international migrants or divorced people. They also often contain older or elderly widows who have outlived their partners. **[Maximum 3 marks]**

Marriage and Divorce

10. D
11. **Example answer:** These official statistics on national divorce rates are from the ONS which is a reputable source. The divorce rates are based on statistics from the courts that deal with and grant divorces. The number of divorces is recorded by following official standards and guidelines. **[1]** So, the data is likely to provide an accurate measurement of divorce. **[1] Other possible strengths:** More valid/reliable than, for e.g., crime rates; generalisation is possible; can identify trends over time – **1 mark for a possible strength and 1 mark for giving a reason why this is a strength.**

12. **Example answer:** Official statistics from the ONS. **[1]** One factor is higher expectations of marriage. This was partly due to the way the media portrayed romance in films and pop songs. So, people were no longer prepared to stay in an empty-shell marriage that did not fulfil them. They were more likely to divorce. **[3] Other possible factors include:** Legal changes; less stigma attached to divorce; impact of secularisation; the changing social and economic status of women – **1 mark for identifying the type of data and 3 marks for explaining a relevant factor.**

Pages 11–16 Education

The Role of Education from a Functionalist Perspective

1. **Example answer:** One function of education is secondary socialisation. **[1]** From a functionalist perspective, schools are an agency of socialisation that promote the norms and values of the wider society. For example, children learn the values of achievement and equality of opportunity at school. These values are important in the wider society. Also, subjects like history instil shared norms and values, and encourage individual children to see themselves as part of society. **[3]** Other possible functions include gender socialisation; economic function; selection; role allocation; facilitating social mobility; fostering social cohesion; social control – **1 mark for a relevant function and 3 marks for explaining this function.**

The Marxist Approach to Education

2. **Possible content: up to 4 marks for AO1; up to 4 marks for AO2; up to 4 marks for AO3.**
   - Define the term capitalism.
   - Argue from a Marxist perspective that the main role of education is to meet the needs of capitalism and to produce a workforce for capitalism. Draw on Bowles and Gintis's correspondence principle to show how education and work connect under capitalism.
   - Draw on Willis's study of the counter-school culture to explain how working-class boys end up in working-class jobs under capitalism.
   - Criticise the Marxist approaches e.g. Bowles and Gintis exaggerate the power of the education system in forming attitudes.
   - Draw on the ideas of Durkheim and Parsons from a functionalist perspective to argue that education has several important functions (e.g. socialisation and role allocation). Argue from a functionalist perspective that the main role of education is to meet the needs of industrial society/the economy.
   - Criticise the functionalist approach e.g. role allocation does not necessarily operate on the basis of talents or abilities.
   - Argue from a feminist perspective that the main role of education is to reproduce patriarchy and gender inequality.
   - Criticise the feminist approach.
   - Reach a balanced conclusion that addresses 'how far'.

Different Types of School

3. **Suggested answer:** One alternative that Illich suggested is deschooling. This involves people becoming truly educated rather than just being schooled. Deschooling would involve abolishing school-based education in its current form. Instead, people could set up learning webs, decide what to learn for themselves and go about learning in creative and exploratory ways. **[Maximum 3 marks]**
4. **Suggested answer:** One criticism is labelling. With the tripartite system, primary school pupils in Year 6 sit an 11-plus exam to assess their aptitudes and needs. Those with the higher scores in the 11-plus go to grammar schools in Year 7 and those with lower scores go to secondary modern schools. This is seen as labelling some pupils as academic 'failures'. These pupils could lose confidence, come to see themselves as failures and stop trying at school. **[Maximum 3 marks]**

Social Class and Educational Achievement

5. **Example answer:** One strength is the relatively large size of the samples. One sample had 2555 students and the other had 19 000 children. **[1]** The research covers a lot of students so the sample is more likely to be representative (compared to a smaller sample) or typical of the wider population of students. **[1] Other possible strengths:** Opinion polls are relatively quick and cheap; drawing on data from several sources; an opinion poll can be replicated to check the reliability of findings – **1 mark for a relevant strength and 1 mark for giving a reason why this is a strength.**
6. **Example answer:** It increased/rose by 7 percentage points. **[1]** One factor is the impact of the economic recession on job opportunities. Following the global recession in 2008 and the limited job opportunities for young people, affluent parents might believe there is more pressure on their children to achieve top grades in their exams to get into a prestigious university and enter a professional career. **[3] Other possible factors:** More testing of students; more pressure to perform well in SATs; more pressure to pass the 11-plus exam/school entrance exam; increased competition within education; more recently, the impact of school closures during the COVID-19 pandemic – **1 mark for describing the change and 3 marks for explaining a relevant factor.**

The Impact of School Processes on Working-Class Students' Achievements

7. **Example answer:** One disadvantage is lack of access to schools to carry out long-term research. **[1]** In a longitudinal study, a researcher would need to return to the school regularly over several years to gather data about the effects of banding e.g. on students' performance or behaviour. A headteacher might be unwilling to allow a researcher to carry out a long-term longitudinal study of banding because it would involve repeat visits, cause disruption or make too many demands on the time of staff and students e.g. during exam periods. **[3] Other possible disadvantages:** time and expense; participants or schools may withdraw from the study; teachers' involvement in a longitudinal study on banding might influence their behaviour in classrooms – **1 mark for a relevant factor and 3 marks for explaining this factor.**

Ethnicity and Educational Achievement

8. B
9. **Suggested answer:** Different exclusion rates: one possible example is that, in some schools, students from particular minority ethnic groups experience higher rates of exclusion when compared to other students in these schools. For example, there are relatively high rates of fixed-term exclusion among students from Black Caribbean backgrounds in some schools, which has been linked to institutional racism. **[Maximum 3 marks]**

Gender and Educational Achievement

10. **Suggested answer:** Some feminists criticise the curriculum because it is gendered rather than unbiased. In a gendered curriculum, some subjects including high-status subjects such as maths and science are associated with masculinity. Other subjects such as humanities and languages are associated with femininity. **[Maximum 3 marks]**

Perspectives on the Counter-School Culture

11. B
12. **Example answer:** One issue is getting informed consent from school children. **[1]** When researching a counter-school culture, the researcher must decide whether the younger students are mature enough to give informed consent themselves. A member of a counter-school culture might want to take part in the study because they like the attention or the idea of appearing in a book but they might not appreciate any possible disadvantages. So, I would ask the students and also their parents/carers to give informed consent (or otherwise). **[3] Other possible issues:** Confidentiality; anonymity; avoiding

harm to participants – **1 mark for a relevant issue and 3 marks for explaining this issue.**

An Introduction to Crime and Deviance

1. **Example answer:** Her Majesty's Prison Service. **[1]** People who are found guilty of committing serious crimes (such as murder) get a prison sentence and are kept in custody for a period of time. Prison operates as an agency of formal social control by punishing convicted offenders and rehabilitating them. It also deters them from reoffending and deters other people from committing crimes. **[3] Other possible agencies:** The legislature; the police; the judiciary; the probation service – **1 mark for a relevant agency and 3 marks for explaining how it operates.**

Functionalist and Interactionist Perspectives on Crime and Deviance

2. **Example answer:** Through participant observation, the researcher can explore the development of deviant careers as they unfold over quite a long period of time. **[1]** A deviant career takes time to develop and involves several stages. By using participant observation, the researcher could join a group of people who have been publicly labelled as deviant. The researcher could participate in their daily activities over time (e.g. a year) to gather data on how and why some of them develop deviant careers while others don't. **[3] Other possible advantages:** Building up trust and rapport over time; getting a more detailed account of the process of developing a deviant career; the researcher can spend time hanging around and listening, rather than asking too many questions; the researcher does not have to rely on people's memories; participant observation can generate valid data – **1 mark for a relevant advantage and 3 marks for explaining this advantage.**

3. **A**

Marxist and Feminist Explanations of Crime and Deviance

4. **Suggested answer:** Some women are controlled in public by the threat of male violence. Women are not more at risk of street violence than other social groups, but they often fear male violence and assault. This fear can act as a control on their behaviour. So, for example, they might not go out alone at night when it is dark because they feel at risk. **[Maximum 3 marks]**

Statistical Data on the Extent of Crime

5. **Example answer:** They ignore the 'dark figure' of crime. **[1]** The dark figure includes crimes that have not been reported to the police because, for instance, victims are too scared to report them or victims think the police won't take them seriously. It also includes unrecorded crimes. These crimes are reported but the police do not record them because, for example, they see them as too petty. So, the statistics do not give a valid or an accurate measurement of all crimes committed. **[3] Other possible problems:** Trends in crime based on these statistics may be inaccurate; the statistics are a social construct; they reflect labelling processes; white-collar and corporate crime are under-represented – **1 mark for a relevant problem and 3 marks for explaining this problem.**

Factors Affecting Criminal and Deviant Behaviour

6. **Example answer:** Confidentiality. **[1]** For example, as a researcher, I would have to consider what I would do about confidentiality if a young offender in a young offenders' institution talked about drugs or violence in the institution. I would deal with this by explaining at the very beginning about the limits of confidentiality. For instance, I would inform them that confidentiality would be guaranteed except in circumstances where someone was at serious risk or in danger. And that, in these circumstances, I would have to pass on the information to the relevant authorities. **[3] Other possible issues:** Informed consent; deception; anonymity; protection from harm – **1 mark for a relevant ethical issue and 3 marks for explaining how you would deal with this issue.**

Other Factors Affecting Criminal and Deviant Behaviour

7. **Example answer:** Fewer controls on women due to their changing position in society. **[1]** There were more social controls or constraints on women's behaviour 40 years ago to deter them from committing crimes. These controls no longer operate so rigidly. Women are now less constrained at home and at work. For example, women's opportunities to commit crime are no longer limited by their role as housewives and mothers. So, women not only have similar legal opportunities to men today – they also have similar illegal opportunities. **[3] Other possible reasons:** The chivalry effect is now less common; women's economic situation and experience of poverty – **1 mark for a relevant reason and 3 marks for explaining this reason.**

8. **D**

9. **Possible content: up to 4 marks for AO1; up to 4 marks for AO2; up to 4 marks for AO3.**
   - Define the terms ethnic group and criminal justice system (CJS).
   - Argue that anti-discrimination legislation such as the Equality Act 2010 exists to protect people from racial discrimination within the CJS.
   - Refer to Ministry of Justice statistics to argue that different ethnic groups have different experiences. For example, black people are more likely than white people to be in prison, relative to their proportions in the population. They are also more likely to be stopped and searched by the police.
   - Argue that crime statistics reflect the way policing is carried out and the bias within the CJS.
   - Argue that evidence of institutional racism within the police (e.g. the Macpherson Report) suggests that different groups are treated differently. However, some commentators reject the idea of institutional racism.
   - Argue from an interactionist perspective that some minority ethnic groups may experience labelling within the CJS.
   - Criticise the interactionist approach/the idea of labelling.
   - Argue from a Marxist perspective that different ethnic groups have different experiences within the CJS. Within law enforcement, certain groups such as black and working-class people are more likely to be targeted. By contrast, crimes committed by the bourgeoisie may often be undetected or unpunished.
   - Criticise the Marxist approach.
   - Argue that individuals' experiences of the CJS can differ depending on their class, gender and age as well as their ethnicity.
   - Reach a balanced conclusion that addresses 'how far'.

The Media and Public Debates over Crime

10. **Suggested answer:** One way is by focusing most crime reports on particular groups and issues, such as illegal immigrants, street crime and benefit fraud. By contrast, the media give much less coverage to corporate crime and tax evasion which are more likely to be committed by powerful groups. So, the media set the focus of public debate on, and get people talking about, some types of crime and some criminals rather than others. **[Maximum 3 marks]**

11. **Suggested answer:** A folk devil is a group (such as mods, rockers, hoodies, punks and boy racers) that is seen as a threat to society's values and treated as a scapegoat. Mods, for example, were a youth subculture who rode scooters such as Vespas and wore smart suits. In the early 1960s, mods were represented in the media as a folk devil or a threat when they got into street clashes with rockers in seaside resorts including Clacton. **[Maximum 3 marks]**

An Introduction to Social Stratification

1. **C**

Different Views of Social Class

2. **D**

Factors Affecting Life Chances

3. **Suggested answer:** Governments have tried to tackle racial discrimination by passing laws to make less favourable treatment based on race in recruitment and promotion at work illegal. For instance, the Equality Act 2010 aims to promote a more equal society and outlaws discrimination based on race in employment. The law also provides a means for people to challenge and stop racial discrimination in the workplace. **[Maximum 3 marks]**

4. **Suggested answer:** Ageism refers to age discrimination or less favourable treatment based on age. It can be found in the workplace. For example, a job applicant with the necessary qualifications and experience is not shortlisted for an interview because they are in their 60s and the employers think they will be too old to learn new ways of working or to fit in with a young team. **[Maximum 3 marks]**

5. **Example answer:** One strength is that the female researcher carried out a form of ethnography by wearing a niqab in public. **[1]** This is a strength because, based on her own experiences on the streets of Leicester and her analysis of the data from this, she could understand more fully how Muslim women experience Islamophobia during their daily lives. **[1] Other possible strengths:** By trying to experience Islamophobia herself, the researcher could build rapport with the Muslim women during the interviews; the researcher could use her experiences to inform the interview questions; the ethnography was covert so there is no observer effect; the researcher does not have to rely solely on what interviewees tell her in interviews; the use of more than one qualitative method of research to build a fuller picture – **1 mark for a relevant strength and 1 mark for showing why this is a strength.**

6. **Example answer:** One weakness is that the ethnography was based in just one city rather than across the UK. **[1]** This is a problem because it may not represent the experiences of Muslim women regarding Islamophobia across the UK. **[1] Other possible weaknesses:** Ethical issues regarding informed consent when doing research in public places; relatively small sample size for the interviews; interviewer bias; interview bias – **1 mark for a relevant weakness and 1 mark for showing why this is a weakness.**

7. **Example answer:** Religious hate crime can affect people's life chances by affecting their health (including their mental health) in a negative way. **[1]** In this case, religious hate crime increased the women's chances of experiencing depression. If they are repeat victims of religious hate crime over time, this could affect their chances of being healthy or ill throughout their lives. **[3] Other possible ways:** Limiting the women's employment opportunities; limiting their opportunities to pursue higher education; contributing to their social exclusion – **1 mark for a relevant way and 3 marks for explaining this way.**

Studies of Affluent Workers

8. D
9. D
10. **Suggested answer:** One type is intergenerational social mobility. This refers to movement, either up or down the social strata, as measured between two generations of a family. For example, intergenerational social mobility would have taken place if the daughter of a cleaner (a working-class job) ended up as a hospital consultant (a middle-class job). **[Maximum 3 marks]**

Wealth, Income and Poverty

11. **Example answer:** From a practical point of view, using official statistics saves time and money because they have already been collected and are readily available. **[1]** National official statistics, e.g. on households below average income, fuel poverty and income inequality, are published regularly and give up-to-date data. They are easy, quick and free to access from government websites. So, researchers can draw on this secondary source of quantitative data on people in low-income households in their research on poverty. **[3] Other**

possible advantages: Provide national data that a researcher would be unable to generate independently; can be used to identify trends in the number of people living in low-income households; can be used to identify groups at risk of poverty; can be used to make international comparisons; can be used in mixed methods research alongside qualitative data – **1 mark for a relevant advantage and 3 marks for explaining this advantage.**

Different Explanations of Poverty

12. **Possible content:** up to 4 marks for AO1; up to 4 marks for AO2; up to 4 marks for AO3.
    *   Define the terms poverty, class and capitalist society.
    *   Argue from a Marxist perspective that poverty results from class-based divisions in capitalist society. For instance, capitalism generates extreme wealth for the bourgeoisie and poverty within sections of the proletariat.
    *   Argue that poverty serves the interests of the bourgeoisie, who can hire and fire workers as needed.
    *   Criticise the Marxist approach.
    *   Argue from a functionalist approach that poverty performs positive functions for some groups in industrial society.
    *   Argue from a feminist approach that poverty results from gender inequality rather than from class-based divisions in society e.g. women are at greater risk of poverty than men due, for instance, to the gender pay gap.
    *   Argue that poverty results from economic factors such as downturns in the global economy or inflation.
    *   Argue that poverty results from the inadequacies of the welfare state rather than from class-based divisions in capitalist society.
    *   Argue that poverty results from individual factors rather than from structural factors linked to capitalism. Draw on individual accounts of poverty such as: the culture of poverty; the cycle of deprivation; Murray's New Right account of poverty, the underclass and welfare dependency.
    *   Reach a balanced conclusion that addresses 'how far'.

Power and Authority

13. **Suggested answer:** One example is kidnappers who take someone as a hostage and demand that the hostage's relatives pay a ransom before they will release the hostage. The kidnappers are exercising coercive power by forcing someone to hand over money against their will by threatening to harm the hostage. **[Maximum 3 marks]**

14. **Example answer:** According to Weber, one type is charismatic authority. **[1]** People obey, support or follow someone with charismatic authority because that person is seen as having extraordinary personal qualities or the power to inspire others. Their charisma can help them to lead and inspire others to bring about social change. Religious leaders such as Bishop Desmond Tutu and political leaders such as Nelson Mandela who fought against Apartheid in South Africa had charismatic authority that inspired others globally. **[3] Other possible types:** Legal rational authority; traditional authority – **1 mark for a relevant type and 3 marks for explaining this type.**

Power and the State

15. **Suggested answer:** From a Marxist perspective, the bourgeoisie hold power over the proletariat in a capitalist society. They have economic power based on their ownership of private property and the means of production such as capital, big businesses, factories and land. The bourgeoisie's economic power gives them political power. They exercise their power to further their own interests rather than the interests of the wider society. **[Maximum 3 marks]**

Pages 30–49 **Practice Exam Paper 1**

Section A: Families

01 D
02 C

03 Suggested answer: One possible consequence is loss of emotional support. Divorce can be emotionally upsetting for all family members. It can be particularly difficult for ex-partners whose social networks change after their divorce. One of the ex-partners may lose their sources of emotional support after they divorce if their friendship groups and kinship networks change. If this happens, it may be difficult to find alternative sources of support. **[Maximum 3 marks]**

04 Suggested answer: One alternative is Kibbutzim in Israel. A kibbutz consists of a group of people who live communally in settlements. The members value equality and cooperation. On some kibbutzim, younger children live with their biological parents and move to the teenagers' houses when they are 15. Each family has its own apartment but usually people eat their meals in the communal dining hall. All children born in the same year are raised and educated together, spending the day in the children's houses. **[Maximum 3 marks]**

05 Example answer: One strength is that the researchers delivered the questionnaire survey by telephone as well as online. This allows people to participate even if they do not have regular access to the internet in their household because, for instance, they are not computer literate. **[1]** This is likely to make the sample more representative of UK households. Without a representative sample, it would be difficult to generalise or to say that the results apply to the wider population. **[1] Other possible strengths:** The longitudinal design allows researchers to explore continuity and change in people's experiences of COVID; the COVID-19 study is part of a large-scale study; questionnaires generate quantitative data and allow measurement – **1 mark for a possible strength and 1 mark for giving a reason why this is a strength.**

06 Example answer: Mothers spent 9 hours more on housework per week than fathers. **[1]** One factor is the continuation of women's double shift. Before COVID-19, many married or cohabiting women worked two shifts by doing a paid job outside the home and also most of the housework and childcare. During the pandemic, this did not change significantly, even when fathers and mothers were both furloughed. Many mothers still spent more time on housework than fathers. **[3] Other possible factors:** Patriarchal nature of families; gender expectations; people's attitudes to gender roles may have changed but their behaviour has not changed significantly – **1 mark for identifying the difference and 3 marks for explaining a relevant factor.**

07 Example answer: A skilled interviewer could explore how parents from different backgrounds respond to each other's views when discussing their experiences of home schooling. **[1]** For example, whether the parents agree on the importance of having funding for resources such as computers, textbooks or private tutors. Also, whether any parents change their minds about, for instance, how much support schools should give. This interaction between parents would provide an extra insight over and above what would be possible in one-to-one interviews with parents. **[3] Other possible advantages:** The ability to explore themes such as home schooling and parents' gender or cultural capital in depth; gathering qualitative data; some participants may feel more comfortable/empowered in a group setting; the focus group may generate new ideas about home schooling – **1 mark for a relevant advantage and 3 marks for explaining this advantage.**

08 Suggested answer: The research is based on secondary sources of information/a literature review. **[1]** Writing from a feminist perspective, Oakley uses pre-existing sources including the work of other sociologists and statistics. She uses the information to provide a critical analysis of the conventional nuclear family, including its financial inequality linked to gender. Oakley contrasts the idea of the conventional nuclear family with the reality and argues that living in conventional families can be stressful. **[3] 1 mark for identifying the research method. Up to 3 marks for describing the method and the perspective.**

09 Example answer: One ethical issue is deception in covert research. **[1]** Care of the elderly could be investigated through covert participant observation (PO) in care settings such as care homes. A researcher could take up the role of part-time, paid care assistant to gather data. But covert PO would deceive residents and staff. This would be unethical because the researcher would be hiding the truth from people in the care setting. So, I would investigate care of the elderly through overt PO in a care home because this would provide rich data and it would be more ethical than covert PO because it is transparent. **[3] Other possible issues:** Causing harm or distress to participants; informed consent; anonymity; privacy; confidentiality – **1 mark for a relevant issue and 3 marks for explaining this issue.**

10 Possible content: up to 4 marks for AO1; up to 4 marks for AO2; up to 4 marks for AO3.
- Define the terms family and capitalism.
- Draw on the Marxist perspective to argue that the family not only serves the interests of capitalism but maintains capitalism over time. For example, through socialisation in families, working-class people learn to accept their lower position in capitalist society and to see the system as fair.
- Draw on the Marxist approach of Zaretsky to argue that the nuclear family has an economic function under capitalism because women, as housewives and mothers, carry out unpaid domestic labour. This is essential to capitalism because it maintains daily life. The system of wage labour relies on women's unpaid domestic labour.
- Draw on Zaretsky's work to link the family to social class reproduction over time. For example, the bourgeois family transmits its private property to the next generation through inheritance. The proletarian family reproduces capitalism's labour force by producing future generations of workers.
- Criticise the Marxist approach e.g. it ignores people's satisfaction with family life; it ignores diversity in families in Britain today.
- Draw on feminist approaches (e.g. the account of Delphy and Leonard) to argue that the family serves the interests of patriarchy rather than capitalism.
- Criticise the feminist approach.
- Draw on functionalist approaches (e.g. Parsons) to argue that the family meets the needs of industrial society and of individuals.
- Criticise the functionalist approach.
- Reach a balanced conclusion that addresses 'how far'.

11 Possible content: up to 4 marks for AO1; up to 4 marks for AO2; up to 4 marks for AO3.
- Define the terms nuclear family and isolated.
- Draw on the functionalist approach (e.g. Parsons) to argue that the nuclear family has become more isolated or separated from the wider family.
- Draw on Young and Willmott's research to argue that the nuclear family has become more separated from the extended family. For instance, fewer daughters see their mothers every day.
- Discuss how geographical mobility and women's increased participation in paid work impact on how often family members see each other and on family ties.
- Draw on Goldthorpe's affluent worker study to argue that families are becoming more privatised and home-centred in their lifestyles. However, Devine's study found that geographical mobility did not necessarily lead to separation from kin or to a home-centred privatised lifestyle.
- Draw on other research (e.g. Charles et al.) to argue that high rates of face-to-face contact between family members can be found. Also, grandparents continue to play an important role in families today e.g. by providing childcare.
- Argue that many families continue to support each other e.g. via financial help or telephone calls, even if they do not meet regularly.

- Argue that it is not useful to generalise about family life in culturally diverse societies such as Britain e.g. the wider family plays an important role among some minority ethnic groups.
- Reach a balanced conclusion that addresses 'how far'.

Section B: Education

12 B

13 A

14 **Suggested answer:** One way is by providing equal opportunities within education as a route to intergenerational, upward social mobility. By working hard at school and going to university, a student from a working-class background could achieve educational success and high-level qualifications. They could then get a top job or enter a profession by becoming a lawyer or a GP. **[Maximum 3 marks]**

15 **Suggested answer:** This refers to the idea that men's traditional masculine identity is under threat. For example, working-class masculine identity was traditionally linked to the breadwinner role and to working in manufacturing and heavy industries (such as shipbuilding). Many jobs in these sectors have declined and working-class men are now more likely to work in low-paid, insecure jobs in the service sector. So, they no longer have such a clear-cut role in society. **[Maximum 3 marks]**

16 **Example answer:** One strength is that the research is based on mixed methods: it combines in-depth interviews with primary heads, a survey of heads and official statistics from the DfE. **[1]** This is a strength because it provides both quantitative and qualitative data. The researchers could draw on statistics from the survey and the DfE, and more detailed accounts from the interviews. This gives both breadth and depth. **[1] Other possible strengths:** The research combines primary and secondary sources; the survey was nationwide; headteachers might be more honest in an anonymous survey; the researchers can use triangulation to cross-check the validity of the findings; the findings might be useful to policy makers; the findings might contribute to future government policy on SATs – **1 mark for a relevant strength and 1 mark for giving a reason why this is a strength.**

17 **Example answer:** One factor is that SATs are high-stakes tests because the results affect a school's position in the performance tables. **[1]** If most pupils do well, this could improve the school's position in the league tables. On the other hand, poor results could lead to an OFSTED inspection. This puts extra pressure on heads to prepare for the tests by setting or by focusing their efforts on borderline pupils in order to get better results. **[3] Other possible factors:** The results are high stake because they are used to compare schools; they are used in the competition to attract parents; parental attitudes to SATs and parents' expectations may influence how schools prepare for the tests; SATs results form part of OFSTED's assessment of a school's quality; some headteachers worry that poor results may lead to them losing their jobs – **1 mark for a relevant factor and 3 marks for explaining this factor.**

18 **Example answer:** The researcher is not fully in control of the process of selecting a sample of the members. **[1]** Snowball sampling means that the researcher may have to rely on the willingness of one member of an anti-school sub-culture to identify other members. This individual might not want to identify others in case they object to talking to an authority figure, distrust them or have better things to do. This means that things like luck or chance can play a part in the sampling process. **[3] Other possible disadvantages:** Sampling could be very time consuming; unlikely to generate a large sample; the sample will not be random/representative/typical of the wider population; the researcher may not be able to gather relevant data; the researcher cannot generalise – **1 mark for a relevant disadvantage and 3 marks for explaining this disadvantage.**

19 **Suggested answer:** Ball used participant observation in a school as his research method. **[1]** He studied banding and mixed-ability teaching at Beachside Comprehensive School to explain the underperformance of working-class students. This

was an ethnographic case study that focused on people in an everyday setting. Ball's perspective is partly interactionist because he explores the interactions between teachers and students but he also pays attention to the wider structure of the school. He is now a leading sociologist who studies social inequality within education and is critical of much government policy on education including marketisation. **[3] 1 mark for identifying the relevant research method. Up to 3 marks for describing this method and Ball's perspective on education.**

20 **Example answer:** One possible expectation is that students in the bottom band will achieve low grades at GCSE. **[1]** If a teacher doesn't expect students in the bottom band to do well academically, this could act as a negative label. It could encourage these students to give up making any effort or striving to improve on their predicted GCSE grades. The teacher could also not put much effort into pushing students in the bottom band to improve their performance. So, low expectations could lead to a self-fulfilling prophecy in that the original prediction comes true. **[3] Other possible expectations:** Expecting students in the bottom band not to complete homework; expecting students to prioritise other aspects of their lives over school work; expecting students to leave school after GCSEs rather than to stay on to study higher level courses; expecting students to obtain low-skilled jobs – **1 mark for a relevant expectation and 3 marks for explaining the impact of this expectation.**

21 **Possible content: up to 4 marks for AO1; up to 4 marks for AO2; up to 4 marks for AO3.**
- Outline the differences in educational achievements between students based on their social class, ethnicity and gender.
- Argue that home background is the most important factor. Examine the influence of possible home-based factors on educational achievement such as: economic circumstances and material deprivation; parental values and expectations; cultural deprivation; peer groups in the neighbourhood.
- Draw on the work of Ball, Bowe and Gewirtz to examine the influence of parents' educational backgrounds and cultural capital on achievement.
- Argue that school-based factors and processes are more important than home-based factors. Examine the influence of factors such as teacher expectations (e.g. Ball), labelling and the self-fulfilling prophecy on different students' educational achievements.
- Examine the influence of school-based factors such as the school ethos and the counter-school culture on the achievement of different students.
- Examine factors such as school-based resources, the quality of teaching, the gendered curriculum, the ethnocentric curriculum and institutional racism on achievement.
- Argue that schools are meritocratic and that educational achievement is linked to individual effort rather than to home-based factors.
- Argue that educational policy is most important. Examine factors linked to policy such as the impact of marketisation (e.g. Ball, Bowe and Gewirtz) on different students and schools; the impact of equal opportunities policies and anti-discrimination legislation.
- Reach a balanced conclusion that addresses 'how far'.

22 **Possible content: up to 4 marks for AO1; up to 4 marks for AO2; up to 4 marks for AO3.**
- Outline the improvements in girls' educational achievements, such as their improved performance in public examinations; increased likelihood of progressing to university. Indicate that subject choices within FE and HE are still gendered.
- Argue that the improvements in attainment are mainly due to changing government policies/legislation, such as the Sex Discrimination Act (1975); the Equality Act (2010) which makes it illegal for educational providers to discriminate on the basis of gender; and the introduction of the National Curriculum which gives girls and boys

equal access to the same subjects. However, gender differences in subject choice persist.
- Argue that the improvements are due to more girl-friendly schooling and changing assessment patterns such as coursework assessment. However, the curriculum is still gendered.
- Argue that these improvements are mainly due to feminism. Examine the impact of feminism on girls' attitudes to education and gender roles; and the impact of feminism in raising girls' expectations regarding careers and financial independence.
- Argue that the improvements are due to teachers' higher expectations of female students and to equal opportunities policies in schools.
- Argue that, despite the improvements, some feminists still see the education system as patriarchal. For example, the hidden curriculum may value conformity and obedience amongst girls more than boys.
- Reach a balanced conclusion that addresses 'how far'.

Pages 50–69 Practice Exam Paper 2

Section A: Crime and Deviance

01 A

02 D

03 **Suggested answer:** The media can amplify or provoke more deviance by reporting on particular incidents, events or groups in sensationalist and exaggerated ways e.g. by exaggerating the threat posed by street fights between mods and rockers in the 1960s. Such coverage could encourage other young people to behave in the ways that the media portray. So, it could result in even more public disturbances. **[Maximum 3 marks]**

04 **Suggested answer:** Sanctions or rewards and punishments are an informal method of social control. Positive sanctions such as praise reward people who behave according to a group's expectations. Negative sanctions punish people who do not conform to these expectations e.g. by gossiping about them or excluding them from the group. **[Maximum 3 marks]**

05 **Example answer:** One strength is that the research is based on multiple methods. **[1]** This is a strength because Swann can get more insight into the women's involvement in aggressive behaviour. For example, she can draw on her own observations of aggression in clubs. And via focus groups, she can see how the women respond to each other's views, and she can also get more insights into their norms and values. **[1] Other possible strengths:** Swann investigated an under-researched topic and shed more light on women's aggressive behaviour; she could cross-check her findings from one method (e.g. interviews) against findings from another (e.g. focus groups); these qualitative methods reduce the imbalance of power between the researcher and the participants; these qualitative methods allow Swann to build up rapport with the women – **1 mark for a relevant strength and 1 mark for showing why this is a strength.**

06 **Example answer:** From an interpretivist approach, it is important to understand people's behaviour by exploring what it means to those involved. **[1]** People could have stereotyped ideas about female violence and aggression. They could see it as mindless, random, unprovoked or less serious than male violence. By getting the women's own accounts, a sociologist can understand their behaviour and how their actions make sense to them. **[3] Other possible reasons:** To get a more valid account of behaviour; so the sociologist can avoid imposing their own meanings on behaviour – **1 mark for a relevant reason and 3 marks for explaining this reason.**

07 **Example answer:** One advantage is that it would provide statistics about people's involvement in anti-social behaviour that was not necessarily dealt with by the police or courts. **[1]** People such as middle-class students might be willing to admit that they have been involved in anti-social behaviour that was not detected or recorded if the study is anonymous and confidential. Respondents have nothing to lose by being honest about their involvement in anti-social behaviour in an anonymous self-report study. **[3] Other possible advantages:** It is possible to compare rates of self-reported involvement by age, gender, ethnicity and social class; can examine whether particular social groups are under-represented or over-represented in police-recorded statistics; useful source in an investigation of the chivalry thesis/institutional racism/the dark figure of crime – **1 mark for a relevant advantage and 3 marks for explaining this advantage.**

08 **Suggested answer:** One response to success goals is innovation. **[1]** In this case, individuals accept the culturally defined goals (such as getting rich) but they lack opportunities to succeed through legal means. So these people innovate by turning to crimes such as theft or fraud to get rich. Merton examined the causes of crime and deviance from a functionalist perspective. He applied the concept of anomie (normlessness) to crime and deviance. He argued that if people experience a mismatch between the goals and the means, then the norms break down and people turn to any means available to achieve economic success. **[3] 1 mark for identifying a relevant response to success goals. Up to 3 marks for describing this response and Merton's perspective on crime and deviance.**

09 **Example answer:** Contributing to social cohesion. **[1]** Social cohesion refers to the idea that people in a society share a set of values and attitudes that help to bind them all together. Crime can contribute to social cohesion e.g. when most people in society react to a violent crime by feeling shocked and outraged. This shared reaction helps to bring people together and reinforces their shared values. As a result, it can reinforce social cohesion. **[3] Other possible functions:** Punishments for crimes reinforce social cohesion – **1 mark for a relevant function and 3 marks for explaining this function.**

10 **Possible content: up to 4 marks for AO1; up to 4 marks for AO2; up to 4 marks for AO3.**
- Define the terms delinquent and sub-culture.
- Argue that sub-cultural theories explain crime and deviance in terms of the values of a particular sub-culture and the influence of a peer group.
- Draw on Albert Cohen's sub-cultural theory to argue that crime and deviance among working-class boys is linked to membership of a delinquent sub-culture and status frustration at school.
- Criticise Albert Cohen's work.
- Draw on Merton's functionalist account of the breakdown of norms (anomie) to explain crime and delinquency.
- Criticise Merton's work.
- Draw on functionalist approaches to argue that inadequate socialisation in families and in schools is the main cause of youth crime and deviance.
- Draw on Marxist ideas to argue that certain groups (such as young people, particularly inner-city and working-class youth) are more likely to be targeted by the police and to be seen as delinquent or deviant.
- Draw on labelling theory and Becker's idea that membership of a deviant sub-culture is just one step in the development of a deviant career rather than the main cause of crime and deviance.
- Criticise Becker's work.
- Reach a balanced conclusion that addresses 'how far'.

11 **Possible content: up to 4 marks for AO1; up to 4 marks for AO2; up to 4 marks for AO3.**
- Outline the gendered patterns of crime shown in police-recorded crime statistics: females commit fewer crimes, less serious crimes and are less likely to reoffend than men. But the number of female offenders is increasing.
- Draw on Heidensohn's feminist account to argue that patriarchal society controls women more effectively than men so it is harder for them to break the law.

- Taking the statistics at face value, as an accurate measure, women may commit fewer crimes because they have less opportunity to offend. For example, their domestic role and triple shift mean they have less time to offend. Females are also more closely controlled than men.
- Taking the statistics at face value, it may be that gender socialisation processes encourage females to be passive and to avoid crime and delinquency.
- Argue that the statistics underestimate the true level of crimes committed by females because the police act with chivalry towards female offenders and treat them more leniently than males. So the police are less likely to arrest and detain female offenders and to record female crime. So, much female crime is part of the 'dark figure' of crime.
- Draw on the double deviance theory to argue that women who commit crime (particularly women who do not conform to feminine stereotypes) are treated more harshly than men.
- Argue that police-recorded crime statistics are socially constructed and underestimate the level of crime committed by females, particularly middle-class females.
- Reach a balanced conclusion that addresses 'how far'.

Section B: Social Stratification

12 B

13 B

14 **Suggested answer:** From a functionalist perspective, Davis and Moore saw social stratification as a way of making sure that the most talented and highly qualified people in society end up in the jobs that are most important to society. This function of matching the most talented people to the most important jobs helps society to run more smoothly. **[Maximum 3 marks]**

15 **Suggested answer:** One example is first past the post. This electoral system is used in general elections to elect MPs to the House of Commons. First past the post is like a race – the candidate who gets the most votes in a particular constituency automatically wins the race and becomes the MP in that constituency. **[Maximum 3 marks]**

16 **Example answer:** Murray only uses official statistics that support his arguments about the underclass. **[1]** For example, Murray didn't use official statistics to show how much of the increase in births outside marriage resulted from the increase in babies born to cohabiting couples. This is a weakness because it suggests a bias in his work. **[1] Other possible weaknesses:** The term 'underclass' is used as a label to blame the people who experience poverty for their misfortunes; the researcher relies on secondary sources and does not collect primary data; the researcher relies on quantitative sources and does not collect qualitative data – **1 mark for a relevant weakness and 1 mark for showing why this is a weakness.**

17 **Example answer:** One way is that governments fail to fund the welfare state adequately because, for example, they think people should take individual responsibility. **[1]** For instance, some critics of government welfare policies and reforms say that the minimum wage and state benefits are too low to meet people's needs. As a result, some pensioners cannot afford to heat their homes in winter and some families have to rely on food banks to feed their children during the school holidays. These critics also argue that governments could end fuel poverty and child poverty by raising the value of state pensions and welfare benefits. **[3] Other possible ways:** From a New Right approach, by encouraging welfare dependency; by creating a culture of dependency; by taking away people's incentive to work – **1 mark for a relevant way and 3 marks for explaining this way.**

18 **Example answer:** Deciding exactly when to measure mobility from. **[1]** Mobility studies have to record movement up or down the social strata between two points in time. Sociologists have to decide which age and point in a person's career to measure mobility from. These decisions are not always straightforward or easy. For instance, a young graduate might be in a temporary job such as in a call centre while they are waiting for a suitable opening in an

investment bank in London. **[3] Other possible problems:** Relying on research participants' memories of their own careers over time; relying on participants' knowledge of their parents' employment histories; earlier studies of inter-generational social mobility often focused on men which could be problematic for researchers who draw on these studies as a secondary source – **1 mark for a relevant problem and 3 marks for explaining this problem.**

19 **Suggested answer:** The method was a large-scale questionnaire survey that was delivered face-to-face by a big team of interviewers across the UK. **[1]** This landmark survey asked about people's household resources and standards of living. Townsend developed a deprivation index to measure the extent of poverty (or relative deprivation) in the UK. He was a pioneer in the study of poverty because he focused on deprivation and viewed it in relative terms. **[3] 1 mark for identifying the relevant research method. Up to 3 marks for describing this research method and Townsend's perspective on poverty.**

20 **Example answer:** One factor is young people's educational qualifications. **[1]** Some young people's access to good-quality, secure employment, good pay or to higher education is limited by their lack of educational qualifications. Many young people without qualifications are likely to wind up in low-paid, insecure jobs or zero-hours contract work. They may struggle to find work if they lack qualifications or skills. **[3] Other possible factors:** Family income e.g. availability of financial help from parents to fund internships; access to social contacts to help young people get work experience; access to adequate, affordable housing; access to health care; whether they experience discrimination e.g. in the labour market; whether they have a disability or ill health – **1 mark for a relevant factor and 3 marks for explaining how this factor might impact on life chances.**

21 **Possible content: up to 4 marks for AO1; up to 4 marks for AO2; up to 4 marks for AO3.**
- Define the terms social class and inequality.
- Draw on Marxist approaches to argue that social class is the most significant source of inequality in capitalist societies. Refer to issues such as working-class educational underachievement and life chances in relation to income, health, housing, social mobility and the under-representation of people from working-class backgrounds in positions of power in Britain.
- Criticise the Marxist approach.
- Argue that ethnicity is the most significant source of inequality. Refer to issues such as racism and institutional racism, average earnings, unemployment, educational underachievement and the under-representation of some minority ethnic groups in positions of power in Britain.
- Argue that some minority ethnic groups are better placed than others, for example in terms of educational achievement, so it is not appropriate to generalise.
- Draw on feminist approaches to argue that gender is the most significant source of inequality in patriarchal society. Refer to issues such as gender inequality at work, the glass ceiling, the gender pay gap, the risk of poverty, sexism and female under-representation in positions of power.
- Criticise the feminist approach.
- Argue that age and disability are the most significant sources of inequality in British society today.
- Argue that all forms of inequality are significant and they should be seen as interrelated or linked rather than as separate aspects.
- Reach a balanced conclusion that addresses 'how far'.

22 **Possible content: up to 4 marks for AO1; up to 4 marks for AO2; up to 4 marks for AO3.**
- Define the term power.
- Indicate that when examining the distribution of power, sociologists focus on who holds power and who exercises it within areas such as politics and the economy. They also look at power relationships within everyday settings such as homes and workplaces.

- Argue that, within everyday settings, power is not shared equally if some groups have power over others.
- Draw on the conflict approach to argue that the distribution of power is unequal. Argue that power is concentrated in the hands of a minority whose members come from privileged backgrounds. Unelected groups such as chief executives of multinational corporations exercise power by influencing government policy.
- Draw on Marxist approaches to argue that power in capitalist society is distributed unequally and this is linked to social class relationships. Members of the bourgeoisie hold power based on their ownership of the means of production. The state protects the interests of members of the bourgeoisie.
- Criticise Marxist approaches.
- Draw on feminist approaches to argue that power is concentrated in male hands in patriarchal society. Discuss Sylvia Walby's work on patriarchy in British society.
- Criticise feminist approaches.
- Draw on the pluralist approach to argue that political power is distributed widely (e.g. through pressure groups, trade unions and direct action groups) and no single group dominates. The role of the state is to regulate the different interests in society.
- Reach a balanced conclusion that addresses 'how far'.

Acknowledgements

The author and publisher are grateful to the copyright holders for permission to use quoted materials and images.

All images © Shutterstock.com

Every effort has been made to trace copyright holders and obtain their permission for the use of copyright material. The author and publisher will gladly receive information enabling them to rectify any error or omission in subsequent editions. All facts are correct at time of going to press.

Published by Collins
An imprint of HarperCollins*Publishers* Ltd
1 London Bridge Street
London SE1 9GF

HarperCollins*Publishers*
Macken House
39/40 Mayor Street Upper
Dublin 1
D01 C9W8
Ireland

ISBN 9780008535070

First published 2017

This edition published 2022

10 9 8 7 6 5 4

British Library Cataloguing in Publication Data.

A CIP record of this book is available from the British Library.

Authored by: Pauline Wilson
Commissioning Editors: Katherine Wilkinson and Charlotte Christensen
Editors: Charlotte Christensen and Shelley Teasdale
Project Manager: Tracey Cowell
Cover Design: Sarah Duxbury and Kevin Robbins
Inside Concept Design: Sarah Duxbury and Paul Oates
Text Design and Layout: Jouve India Private Limited
Production: Karen Nulty
Printed in the UK, by Ashford Colour Press Ltd.